The
Big Brother's
Guide to
Networking

The Big Brother's Guide to Networking

DR. DAVID A. BISHOP

NVR Publishers

Contact: New York Research Publishers

http://www.nyrpublishers.com

Copyright © 2018 David A. Bishop

All rights reserved.

ISBN-13 978-0-9998160-0-4

ISBN-13 978-0-9998160-1-1

DEDICATIONS

To all of my mentees, I hope this helps you become a better networker, and enriches your personal and professional life.

TABLE OF CONTENTS

CHAPTER ONE

INTRODUCTION:
WHY I WROTE THIS BOOK

A few years ago, I decided to give back to my community by volunteering at my alma mater to mentor college students. I worked with young people from all over the world at various stages of professional development. I spent time with both graduate and undergraduate students to understand their fears, concerns, hopes, and dreams, and how I could help them, at least in some small way, along the path to success. I soon realized there was a serious gap in how we mentor and lead our young people. Although some had access to good advice at home, many students were lost and lacked the experienced guidance that some of us take for granted. I thought back to my own youth and remembered how the gaps in my knowledge that made decision making difficult. Decisions made early in life can have long-standing impacts, and at that age we don't always have access to the knowledge (of the world or of ourselves) to make the right decision. To a certain extent, we all go through this, but I thought to myself, wouldn't it be wonderful if we all had a big brother who could sit down with us, cut through the fog of youth, and give us the straight dope on what we needed to know to decide for ourselves? Knowing how to navigate common problems, avoid pitfalls, and do things to make life easier could be very helpful. Many people have a big brother, parent, or similar mentor at home who helps them through these things, but many don't. Even if they do, such mentors usually don't have the professional or industry level knowledge needed by today's young people. That's why the Big Brother series of books was created: To provide people with a big brother in their pocket they could turn to for advice on common problems, maladies, and situations of transitioning into and working professionally. The focus is on providing the candid, no-nonsense knowledge that you won't get in a typical book on the topic. Rather, The Big Brother series seeks to provide uncommon knowledge. The kind that only a caring mentor with only your benefit in mind would give. Big Brother books are not just for young people, either. During my research, I also discovered that just about everyone needs a big brother. I think we all could use one at various points throughout our lives.

During my experience as a mentor, I found that most recent college graduates are concerned about getting their first job. With many newly minted graduates facing huge student loan debts, the pressure is on to jump right into the workforce soon. In working with them, the most common question I got was, "How do I network with people?" Many struggle with this topic, and so I thought it was worth writing a book on. Understanding what networking is, how it works, what it can and can't do, and how to leverage it, is an art form usually learned through experience. I've seen people who are naturals at it, but few. In this book, you will learn all you must know about networking and how to use it to get your next job. It's that simple.

CHAPTER TWO

BASIC PRINCIPLES OF NETWORKING

When most people think of networking, they think of going to meetings, introducing themselves and building a contact who could eventually land them a job or business. However, networking is much more than that, and research studies have revealed that the most effective kind of networking works much differently than we think. In this chapter, I will discuss some of this research and how you can integrate it into your networking strategy.

In the early 1970s, a researcher and sociologist at John Hopkins University (later, Stanford University), Mark Granovetter, published a body of research titled "The Strength of Weak Ties." In this landmark paper, Granovetter wanted to discover what role networking played in getting jobs. His findings were surprising. Although most people got jobs through networking contacts, most jobs were obtained with contacts that the job changer did not know well. According to the study, less than 17% of the jobs were found through a contact that the job changer talked to often (Granovetter 1973). The clear majority of jobs were obtained with contacts the job seeker either only occasionally or rarely had contact with. This strength in weak ties belied the often-held concept that jobs are obtained primarily through people we know well and have close relationships with. Rather, the contrary is true. Research shows us that most jobs are not obtained through close contacts, but via people we barely know. These weak ties we have with people serve as a conduit or grapevine of sorts through which we hear about new opportunities. When Granovetter asked respondents whether a friend had told them about their current job, they often replied, "Not a friend, an acquaintance." (Granovetter 1973). With many of the job seekers, this contact was someone on the fringe of their contact list, such as a former co-worker or college friend with whom only sporadic contact had been maintained over the years. Such contacts were found to not even be very strong when they were first created. Also discovered was the path through which the jobs were found. Most often, these paths were short, meaning that either the friend or acquaintance in question got the job information directly from the employer with whom the job seeker was already familiar, or there was only one intermediary involved.

Granovetter's research tells us that to improve your chances of getting a job, you should focus not so much on building close relationships with a select group of people, but build acquaintances with as many people as possible working for or doing business with companies that interest you. So, to get a job, this changes the entire nature of what networking is all about and what it means to most people. Developing close relationships may not be necessary. Granovetter's work became the basis for the success of today's online social networks, which we will discuss later.

Lessons learned about the true nature of networking:

1. Openly network with people online and socially. Limiting the people, you connect to will limit your possibilities. One of the biggest mistakes I've seen others do is refuse a connection on social media because they don't know the person well or remember them, as if your relationships on these sites should consist of only the closest of ties. How closed-minded this is!

2. Maintain old contacts. School chums, old co-workers, etc. Don't go to lunch with them every week, but drop them a line occasionally and say hi. Connect to them on social media. It's important to maintain these contacts.

3. Target companies that hire your kind of expertise and seek contacts that work there.

4. Although not necessarily required, developing close relationships can play a part in your job search strategy, just don't make it your primary focus.

Close relationships may not be as critical regarding employment, but they can be very important in other contexts where the stakes are higher so to speak. In the next chapter, we will explore the art of meeting new people.

CHAPTER THREE

MEETING NEW PEOPLE

How to approach someone you don't know

When working with my students, many seemed to have the hardest time figuring out how to approach someone they didn't know. It's very much like asking someone out on a date, which a lot of young people still have trouble with in their 20s. Heck, I think there's probably a lot of 40-year-olds that get cold feet asking a person out! Whatever your age or position, there is a certain way you can approach someone you don't know that can ensure success in starting a new friendship, without looking like a goof! And yes, you could use this technique to ask someone out on a date, not just business.

First, let's start with what you don't do. Don't use silly one-liners, bump into someone and make them drop their books, or pretend you think you know them from somewhere. It's best to meet people in a forum based on a common interest (no, not a bar). Examples include conferences, club meetings, or a special gathering or event. This could be a basis for your introduction.

Getting Started – Initiating Contact:

1. Establish your targets.

2. Gather intelligence on them.

3. Create a short elevator introduction for yourself and tie it to the special common interest of the event you're attending or the intelligence you gathered. Try to find one piece of information about that person which could kick off the conversation.

4. Act with confidence. Wait for a free moment when the person is not preoccupied, and simply walk up and introduce yourself with a firm handshake. Have direct eye contact and smile. Smiling is especially important if you are of the opposite sex.

5. Get someone to introduce you if you can.

Once you've established contact, the last thing you want to do is say something like, "Hey, I like that tie you've got on, can you get me a job?" Becoming a conversationalist is an art unto itself, but it's not as hard as you may think. I utilize a four-step approach to doing this.

Making Conversation:

1. People love to talk about themselves. Get them to do so.

2. Follow this by taking a genuine interest in them and what they have to say.

3. Listen and analyze. Pinpoint their interests and desires.

4. Ask questions. Focus on what you're hearing to create your queries.

If you follow these four steps, especially the first two, the conversation will evolve naturally. People can tell if you're faking it. Networking works best when you are gathered in a forum that interests you, you'll have common interests with the target person. Build on that. Talk about what drives you, and that will drive the conversation and create interest and enthusiasm with your target. Make your target feel like you're someone they would want to know. People love to talk about themselves, so ask questions about what they do, their families, and what they enjoy. Try to discover their passions. More important, try to determine their wants and needs, as these will motivate them more than anything else will. If you can translate what you offer to satisfy some want or need your contact has, this is the holy grail. Observe any special characteristics of their dress, jewelry, tattoos, or other accoutrements that would indicate a certain lifestyle, family, hobby, or other interests. If you have some knowledge about the person, use that. For example, "I heard you liked to skydive." Also, use the gathering or common interest as a segue. Try to get into the person and get to know them. This will show, and your new contact will appreciate it and hopefully reciprocate. If they don't, simply move on to the next person you've targeted. Mastering this may take practice. Just like learning to swim, you've got to dive in and try. Don't worry if you flop out a couple times. Everyone does, and it is probably much more noticeable to you than the people around you. Remember that everyone is human, we all have distractions, worries, and concerns. Many times, I thought I struck out with a contact only to have them walk up to me later with a smile and conversation as if nothing bad had happened. When you're speed networking, it's sometimes easy to misinterpret social cues or make incorrect assumptions. Every contact is a good contact. Sometimes just getting your name out there and passing your card along is good enough, or better than nothing. You never know who might call on you later, and you may be surprised when it happens. Understand that every networking session is a good session. Every time you're getting your name and face out there it is a positive thing. So, you didn't get a lot of follow-ups or meet anyone that interested you. Forget about that and move on to the next event. Networking is a numbers game, and there's always more fish in the sea!

Lessons learned:

1. Be observant. Notice who your targets talk to, how they dress, and what they are talking about the most.

2. Be a good listener. Often, people will think you're a great conversationalist even if you have said little, just because you

listened to them and appeared interested.

3. Make your target the topic of conversation. Use what they give you to ask questions and further the conversation.

4. End with a contact or follow-up. Get their card or give them yours, and follow up with an email or phone call a day or two later. Connect on social media.

CHAPTER FOUR

SOCIAL NETWORKS

Theoretically, social networks could be any organization or association that links people, as in Granovetter's work. However, in today's world, social networking has become synonymous with online social networking sites. When I talk about social networks, I'm primarily referring to services such as Facebook, LinkedIn, etc. Online networking is an integral part of life today, and although it has become largely ubiquitous, especially with young people, some are still resistant to using it. Simply, I think you must. If you don't have accounts with these services, you're behind the curve and need to get them. Even online job postings have largely supplanted the newspaper as the primary source for new opportunities.

So, the first question I am often asked, is which networking site is the best? Well, each service has its function and primary focus. Facebook has often been all things to all people. A way for friends and family to keep in touch but also for businesses to promote themselves. Instagram, Pinterest, and many of the other sites are nice, but are not as largely used in the professional business world for making contacts. You can become easily overwhelmed with the plethora of social networking sites and keeping up with them all can be a chore. Before you know it, you'll be spending all day on Facebook or Twitter and lose grip with having a real life. Don't do that! Pick one or two sites and focus on those. I have accounts on all, but I can tell you that unless you have a business to promote, or are a celebrity, focus on Facebook and LinkedIn.

LinkedIn is by far the most popular site for professional networking. If you're looking to get a job, especially in the technology business, you must set up a complete profile on this site. Using the concepts from Grannoveter, try to network with as many people as possible. You don't have to know everyone. Just find people with common interests or those who work for companies you're targeting. You will find that most people are happy to openly network with you. I grew my connection list from 400 to over 4000 followers quickly using this approach. Let me say I have no special interest in LinkedIn financial or otherwise. I'm simply giving you my direct opinion based on experience.

So how do you approach others on social networking sites like LinkedIn? Well, the system allows you to connect using a generic message, something to the effect of "Hi, I'm Mr. X, and I'd like to add you to my network." I don't use any message when I do this. Most of the time, when I send a connect request the person either remembers me from a recent event or can tell from my profile that I work in their industry and I'm someone they would like to know. I've found that works with most people. If they see that you have a professional-looking profile and that you have similar interests or background, they will usually accept. If you have an incomplete profile, no picture, and little information about yourself, be prepared for disappointment.

Sites Like LinkedIn also have features where you can apply for jobs. Applying for jobs can be time-consuming these days because most employers want more than your resume up front, they redirect you to a website to put in your application, which can be several pages long and take hours to complete properly. To get around this, many sites have a "quick apply" option which allows you to simply send the recruiter your profile and attach a copy of your resume. This is quick, easy, and allows you the bandwidth to send several requests in a short time, but I must tell you that I've had little success using this feature. Most companies still want you to apply on their website using their time-consuming application. You need to use LinkedIn to locate new opportunities and identify a contact person for them. Apply for the job officially on their website, and then contact the contact. This method is much more effective. Since filling out these applications can be so time-consuming, you must carefully target your job opportunities.

Once you've built up a good contact list on LinkedIn, you can post articles to promote yourself. Keep these articles simple, straightforward, and professional. Yes, a controversial issue could go viral and get yourself more attention, but be mindful of your goals. Potential clients, business partners, and employers will see your posts. That goes for any social networking site you use. If it's something you don't think everyone should see, don't post it.

If you have time to focus on only one site for professional networking, use LinkedIn. However, Facebook runs a close second. It's no secret that human resources departments and hiring managers frequently browse for Facebook profiles whenever considering a new hire. They will look at your pictures, recent posts, and friends. There are a few security levels to limit access to certain parts of your profile by someone not friended, but the more open you are, the more trust you will build. If you have any politically incorrect posts, those could be bad for you. I usually limit my posts to family pictures, church events, and hobbies. If one of your hobbies is bombmaking, that might not be a good idea though! Be mindful that posts about guns, certain political views, and other non-PC content will often be flagged by these sites and cause you to lose your account or have even worse consequences. You can't be arrested for exercising your right to free speech, but you can lose your job, your home, your family, online accounts and everything else because of it, which effectively means you have no free speech today. Sad but all too true.

Once you get into a workplace, you may find that even though you're connected to most of your co-workers via LinkedIn, many of the "coolest people" are friended together on Facebook, sometimes even in secret or private forums I discovered that all my executives at one company were all hooked up on Facebook and having a good ole time. It was a workplace defined by clichés. We leave high school, go to college to become professionally educated, and then at some point believe we are professionals. However, at some companies, it is not uncommon to find high school-level conduct among executives, with underlings forced to pay homage to the "cool kids" in the most popular cliques. Fall out of favor with these people, and your career will forever suffer, regardless of performance. That's another topic altogether, though!

One way to break into these clichés is to use the "snowball method." The snowball method is a research technique for locating stakeholders. If you must conduct a survey or interview a certain group of people, but you don't know where to start, just start with one person. Ask that person who they know that could help with whatever task you're working on, or simply who would be interested in knowing more about a certain topic you're discussing or promoting. Invariably this person will rattle off a list of people you can contact and ask the same questions. They will give you even more contacts. Before you know it, you will have a huge list of people that have a common interest you can use as a reason to contact them, introduce yourself, and build relationships. You can do this personally via email or phone, but just as easily through Facebook or LinkedIn. It won't be long before you're connected to the inside cliques with the cool kids. Because of this activity, you will be viewed as an insider rather than an outsider, and will, therefore, be within the circle of trust. Breaking into these cliques will help create opportunities for you that you would otherwise not even know about.

CHAPTER FIVE

CLUBS AND PROFESSIONAL ORGANIZATIONS

Getting to know someone often starts with common interests. What do you both like to do in your spare time? What are your interests or passions? Clubs and professional organizations are an excellent way to find people with the same interests as you. These could be alumni associations, professional organizations such as IEEE or ACM, or even Freemasonry. Your place of worship could be a source.

Professional organizations are not only sources for new contacts, they are also sources for new technical information and current events. It's at these meetings where you're most likely to discover new jobs, business opportunities, or even technical information about a common interest. And they are also a means by which you can maintain the contacts you have. In Granovetter's work, he cited this may be the most important function of such meetings.

Although all the organization types I mentioned can have value, the more specific the organization is to your specialties and interests, the more valuable the contacts and your participation will be. There is a professional organization or club for just about anything and everything out there, no matter how narrow the topic may be. I encourage you to search and seek out such organizations that meet your needs and participate heavily.

Volunteering can also be a source. If you frequently volunteer for a charity, this could be a place for you to meet people. Volunteering with people helps build comradery and a common bond. It establishes you as a good person and builds trust. You never know who you may meet, either.

Just a few examples of societies and organizations:

- IEEE
  - ◊ Consists of innumerable sub-societies on many specialties.
- ACM (Association for Computing Machinery)
- IEC (International Electromechanical Commission)
- Alumni Associations
- Religious organizations
- Benevolent societies
- Fraternities/Sororities
- Bar associations
- Jaycees
- Rotary Clubs
- Veterans Organizations

To get the most out of these organizations, you must be more than a participant, you must be engaged, and the more the better. Visibility in these organizations can garner you more contacts and professional prestige. They can take up a lot of time though, so you must balance your involvement with your career objectives and other responsibilities. We will discuss this more in the next chapter.

CHAPTER SIX

SELF PROMOTION TECHNIQUES

If you feel you have plenty of connections and want to take your network to the next level, one way to do it is by promoting yourself. Using self-promotion techniques can help position you as a leader. As a leader or expert in a specific niche or organization, people will seek YOU out for networking. There are many strategies you can use to obtain this status. Let's discuss them.

Volunteering for Leadership Roles

In the previous chapter, we talked about the importance of clubs and professional organizations, and even discussed volunteering or helping out. One way to set yourself apart from the crowd is to volunteer for a leadership position within one organization. Doing so automatically establishes you as a leader and a reliable and responsible person. People within your organization will have less resistance for recommending you for jobs or other opportunities in their own companies. It's not as hard as you may think, either. Most people are too busy or too lazy to take on leadership roles within professional organizations. Competition is typically not that fierce. Try to locate a specialized community you're interested in and run for an officer's role when it becomes available. Better yet, charter a new organization around your specialty if there isn't one.

I once chartered a new professional organization. I started it from scratch and was lucky to get enough votes to establish our charter. Shortly thereafter, I came down with a serious illness, putting a stop to getting the group going. Once I recovered, I picked up the pieces and moved forward. It wasn't easy. Only one person showed up for my first meeting. But for the next meeting we had fourteen show up, and after that, I had volunteers for treasurer and vice chair. Soon, we had a thriving community. It just took perseverance, and belief in what I was doing. I was championing technical startups, which was a passion, and when others saw this, it was contagious. Even people who had no previous interest in startups wanted to be a part of the team because it piqued their interest. They found themselves exposed to possibilities they had not considered.

Volunteer Leadership can accomplish the following:

1. Establish you as a leader or expert in your field.

2. Build trust.

3. Position you as a smart, reliable, and responsible person.

4. Position you as someone who cares about the greater community.

5. Give you a platform you can use to sell yourself or show how smart you are, within boundaries. Don't go overboard here!

Publications

Acting as a writer or editor for a publication, or simply creating articles online for a blog or LinkedIn, can help establish many of the tenets above that being a volunteer/leader can. Try to find a trade publication, or even a blog or online newsletter concentrated on your specialty. If you cannot find one, create it! As you write articles, you'll find that people will respond and want to connect with you. You will always have those that disagree. Many people shy away from this kind of self-promotion because they fear backlash or putting themselves out there. You simply cannot have that attitude. You must let go of your fear. Don't be afraid to be visible! Many of us are introverts and so none of this activity comes naturally to us, we must work at it. But if you take that first step, you may find it opens doors for you that will pay dividends for the rest of your life. Leave your comfort zone and do it!

Public Speaking

Public speaking is one way to get yourself noticed, however, you may not be asked to do this until you have established some credibility or notoriety. This can be done with publications or volunteer leadership. Embrace these opportunities when they come to you. Connect on social networks with everyone you meet. Don't be shy around people that want to get to know you.

CHAPTER SEVEN

THE OTHER SIDE OF NETWORKING

In your professional life, sometimes people will seek you out to network with you, most often, hoping to get a job. As humans, we want to help people, and it is natural for most of us to do as much as possible for someone in need, especially if it is a friend. Unfortunately, there is a downside to referring people for a job, and after understanding what some potential pitfalls are, you can see why many people are reluctant to do so.

I once referred a friend to my manager at the time from a previous employer. "Sam" as I will call him, had over ten years of experience in the IT business with a great reputation at the telecom company where I had worked. I remembered Sam as a tenacious and careful problem solver, well respected within the group we worked together in. I had relied on Sam numerous times to help resolve issues I was working on. It could have easily been said that he was close to being the top person in that group. I had complete confidence in him, with no qualms at all referring him to my new employer when a slot became available.

I was in for a shock.

Sam did great in the interview and got the job. Our new positions in the airline business were different from the Unix system administration jobs we held previously. It was more application oriented, particularly web application oriented. I had spent quite a bit of time learning web apps and explained to my boss this is something Sam would have to pick up. Sam understood too, that he had some learning to do. I didn't realize just how hard that would be for him.

To make a long story short, Sam struggled. He came to me frequently for help and I had no qualms at all helping him, the problem was that he seemed to catch on slowly. I constantly had to show him the same things repeatedly, and he never seemed to take initiative when given new projects. He was so intimidated that he would often try to get someone to do the work for him, explaining, "I don't know how to do this stuff." I tried to assure him that many of us didn't know how to do it at first, only by the act of doing will you learn. It's OK not to know, but it's not OK to pass your work onto others. Sam was not one to fear asking questions either and would ask very basic questions about web apps in group meetings. Some of the more unfriendly people on the team made fun of Sam. He was of Middle-Eastern descent, and although Americanized, there were slight cultural and language barriers. Sam had never been in such a competitive environment before. Our old organization had been low key, which I had forgotten.

I soon realized that one reason Sam had done so well at our old company was that he had been there so long. I never thought he would have so much trouble picking up new skills. I tried to help him as much as I could, but I frequently became frustrated with him, and embarrassed. I was afraid that he was a bad reflection on me with management and that his incompetence and ineptitude would result in failure for him. He had a rough go of it for a while, one project manager and one co-worker picked on him frequently. However, Sam was mature and easy going. He stood his ground. Eventually, time took over and some of the negative people left and were replaced by positive ones.

After several months, Sam showed his strong suits. He was a wiz at scripting and programming. A newly hired lead in the group hailed his skills in front of everyone saying, "Sam is a scripting guru!" "Sam is the man!" Sam's easygoing nature, maturity, and willingness to help people made others comfortable in asking him questions. He became one of the go-to people in that group. It felt good to hear others brag about him. He had a few successes in later projects and his abilities shined through. Long after I left, Sam remained there working, and outlasted all the negative people that made life difficult for him initially.

Little did I know that one day I would be in Sam's shoes. I was working at another telecom when work there became unbearable. Virtually everyone was looking for a way out. It's hard to describe sometimes just how bad a place can get, and this place was bad … and indescribable! When one friend left to go back to his old company and offered to take me with him, I jumped at the chance. Another friend had already gone back. A cool job at another more stable telecom with two ready-made friends already there? What could be better?

Again, I was in for a shock.

The job was great, but I had been a web architect for four years. The Unix admin work in this group was totally system oriented. No applications here! Disks, disks, and more disks! SAN, NAS, the whole nine yards. I loathed disk management but had forgotten just how much. Although I had supported HP servers before, that was years ago. I didn't realize how much I had forgotten. Plus, the fact that the hardware had changed so much. The administrator also served as the data center tech and janitor. I simply didn't realize just how much I had forgotten. Initially, it was a struggle, but I worked hard to learn. It came back and I was up and running within a few weeks and learned bit by bit as I went along. The manager was pleased with my work. However, my so-called friends were not. When I couldn't remember a couple of commands, one of them freaked out, and told my other friend about my failings. I suddenly remembered Sam at my old job and thought of how he must have felt. My friends seemed to lose confidence in me, the weird thing was that they began openly criticizing me and seemed to be taking the initiative to get rid of me! I couldn't understand this logic, and my stress level peaked. They were so paranoid and insecure about their own reputations, they were afraid that I would make them look bad. They took every measure to distance themselves from me. Having a former close friend that you've relied upon for so long as an enemy is very uncomfortable and unnerving. You feel violated and vulnerable. Attacked from all sides. I lost sleep, patience, and sanity. I was a contractor, not a permanent employee, which made my life even more difficult. To make a long story short, I did well in the job and recovered from my failings, but not from the damage it did to my friendships. Honestly, this experience also made me realize that it was time for a career change. I would no longer be happy doing this kind of work. That's another story altogether, though!

If you refer someone to a position within your company, remember that they are human. They aren't perfect. And just because they did well at one place doesn't mean they'll be great at another. They must learn and grow just like you! They might not be a wiz at first, heck, nobody is! Remember that long term, you will cultivate a long, loyal friendship within your company. And what could be worth more than that? That's the reason we refer our friends anyway.

Recommendations

Often, if you're hoping to attend graduate school, professional school, or get a job in academia, recommendations are not important, they are necessary. Few things are more frustrating to a professor or teacher when they are asked for a recommendation on a student they barely know. If you believe that soon you will need recommendations, don't wait until when you need it to get to know the professor. Start early. Cultivate the relationship. Good grades will help, but grades alone will not always get you the glowing recommendation you may need. As with anything, common interests are key. Target professors that are interested in the topics you are. At the beginning of the term, cultivate a relationship using the techniques discussed in previous chapters. If after class or office hours don't permit it, most professional organizations have student branches that are attended to or monitored by professors. These could be venues for networking. It need not be so personal, though. Remember the strength of weak ties. Make good grades and do just enough extra to get yourself noticed. Participate a LOT in classroom discussions, and don't be afraid to speak out. Even if you're wrong about something, your participation will be appreciated. Just don't be monotonous about it. Do a little participation every class. But don't jump in every five minutes. Visibility is what counts.

Professional References

Many of the same rules apply to professional references, if you need them. Decent work performance and a positive relationship with your boss may be all you need for a good professional reference or recommendation. If it's glowing, that's good, but it need not be. Positive is enough. Often, human resources departments are only looking for problems, so if they get the letters or references they need without issue then you're good. One point to note is that many companies don't allow managers or supervisors to refer employees. This is because if the manager says something negative, which is often based on opinion anyway, it could be construed as slander and the company could be put at legal risk. Many companies only allow managers to provide dates of employment and job titles for the person(s) in question. Even salary information is often forbidden. In some companies, the manager may be forced to refer the inquiry to human resources and not say anything. Before you leave any job, discover what the rules are for your company, and properly arrange with your boss on whether they can expect a call or not. These kinds of references are not as important as they once were, as most companies know that they are not reliable anyway. But it does not hurt to make the proper arrangements. Again, in these instances HR is only probing for problems, so a glowing reference holds little weight usually.

CHAPTER EIGHT

NETWORKING DO'S AND DON'TS

When networking with people, there are common do's and don'ts I want to make clear. Although I may have alluded to many in the previous chapters, I'm calling these items out here to make sure you understand them. If you read nothing else in this book, you should at least read and understand this chapter.

List of Do's

1. Set up your LinkedIn profile and connect with people.

2. Connect with as many people as you can. The biggest mistake I see people making is refusing contact with someone because they don't know them well. This is the stupidest thing anyone can do. Remember Granovetter's strength of weak ties. That's the whole purpose of social networking sites. If you aren't connecting, then why are you there?

3. Smile!

4. Dress well, but not over the top for the occasion.

5. Have good hygiene.

6. Act with confidence.

7. If you're attractive, use it to your advantage, but be mindful of the boundaries. If you're unsure, then don't.

8. Post articles of interest on LinkedIn or other social platforms.

9. Avoid family-style events. When there are spouses and children around, it's hard to talk business. Do these for fun, but not for networking.

10. Remember the strength of weak ties.

11. Be a specialist. No one wants a MacGyver type person. If you try to be everything to everyone you will appear superficial. Focus on your strong suits and career interests.

List of Don'ts

1. Make it obvious that you're trying to get to know someone just to use them.

2. Ask for favors or help right away. Give it time.

3. Make mindless conversation about a person's clothing or the car they showed up in, unless you're sincere and love the car!

4. Be rude. Be nice to everyone no matter who they are even if you think they can't help you. You never know who their friends might be. Word gets around.

5. Self-deprecate. Some people think this is desirable in a social context because it shows humility. Most people don't like it. Don't put yourself down under any circumstances.

6. Ignore the social context of where you are. Don't make dirty jokes at a church function.

7. Ignore the culture where you are. If you're in a foreign country or organization, be mindful of the cultural

expectations within those groups. Certain characteristics celebrated in a western context could be frowned upon elsewhere.

8. Promote yourself with relentless Facebook posts. No one cares about what you had for dinner last night.

9. Try to be something you're not. If you don't like computers don't attend an event for computer jockeys. Your attempts at networking will appear insincere and superficial.

CHAPTER NINE

SUMMARY

Networking can often be the key to success in the business world. Whether it's trade group events, professional associations or informal networking, research tells us networking works, so here are our tips on beginning those conversations, nurturing relationships, and following up successfully.

1. Practice Makes Perfect

Don't wait until you need to network, network now. It can be uncomfortable and even daunting to walk into a room full of strangers and be expected to engage. Going to networking events before you need to means you get the practice, without the pressure. It'll give you time to get the feel of a networking event, how you're expected to behave and pick up tips from how others interact.

If you're nervous about the prospect of chatting with strangers, then don't be afraid to prepare. Make yourself some brief notes, ice breaker questions, key points about you or your business and keep them with you at the event. Chances are, you probably won't need to use them, but knowing they're there will be a great comfort.

Discovering who the attendees will be is another tried and tested method. That way you can research about the people you'd like to contact, and you'll be able to converse with them on the day.

Think about starting with people you already know as an 'in.' Contacting people with a referral name you can drop in can help to start the conversation. Likewise, attending your first networking event with someone you already know can greatly aid confidence and help widen your circle. Once you've built a relationship with someone, future contact will get easier and easier. Remember the snowball technique!

2. Have a Plan, Not an Agenda

If you go to an event solely to net clients, it will be obvious and you'll most likely be avoided. Try to go with the view of building relationships and introduce people who may be able to help each other. If you're generous and not self-serving, you're more likely to be the person that people want to talk to and make it more likely that they'll return the favor, if you need it in future.

Try not to obsess about what you want to say. Having something memorized word for word will sound rehearsed and insincere. This is especially important for chats over the phone; you don't want to sound like you're ringing from a call center with a pre-prepared script. Coming back to having notes, try making bullet points on the topics you want to cover and important things you want to remember. That way, if you're asked a question or the conversation slightly changes topic, you won't lose your place or panic.

Don't turn your chat into a sales pitch or you could give out hundreds of business cards and never receive a call. If you think there's a possibility of getting work, then get the contact information of that person and think about dropping them an email the next day rather than putting them on the spot at the event.

3. Engage and Cultivate Relationships

You only get one chance to make a first impression, so make it count. Try to relax, even if you're nervous; fake it. Smile, make eye contact and try to use the person's name in conversation. People like to know you're giving them your full attention, so listen and ask encouraging questions. By doing this, you're also relieving the pressure from yourself as you can encourage them to lead the conversation without having to say much.

Never ask something from someone you just met. If you know someone would be a great 'in' at a company or could put you in touch with the right people, resist asking outright – it's what you'll be remembered for. Instead, try and cultivate that relationship; invest in the person and wait until the time is right before asking for favors. You never know, they may actually be the one to suggest what it is you want.

4. Follow Up and Stay in Touch

Following up on conversations promptly is the key to maintaining a good contact and potentially getting business. If weeks slip by, then the impetus is gone and so is your hard work. If you've got someone interested or excited about your ideas, then strike while the iron's hot. Don't just reiterate what you've already told them, build on it, add something new, or suggest a meeting to follow up on what you talked about.

Following up isn't just for potential clients either. If someone has introduced you to someone else, let them know how the connection is going. Or, drop them an email to thank them for the introduction. Keeping yourself front of mind is no bad thing and it's especially important to keep trying to be in contact when you need nothing. If you only call or email when you want a favor or to sell something, then you'll quickly find your communications going unanswered. If you see an article that might interest a contact, send it; if they send business your way or put a job offer your way, think about sending a thank you card. Little touches like this will maintain relationships and keep opportunities coming your way.

Conclusion

Good and effective networking requires conversation and the ability to invest in and maintain relationships. Going into a networking situation with the mindset of getting to know people and helping others rather than getting leads for yourself will help immensely with gaining trust and developing meaningful contacts.

With sites like LinkedIn, we don't even have to leave the house or make a call to network, so explore every opportunity. Be an open networker, and grow your contact list. Don't forget to maintain relationships. Once you get to know a contact, keep in touch, and follow up on any conversations and hopefully, soon you'll have a wide, communicative networking circle.

REFERENCES

Granovetter, Mark S., American Journal of Sociology, Volume 78, Issue 6 (May 1973), 1360-1380

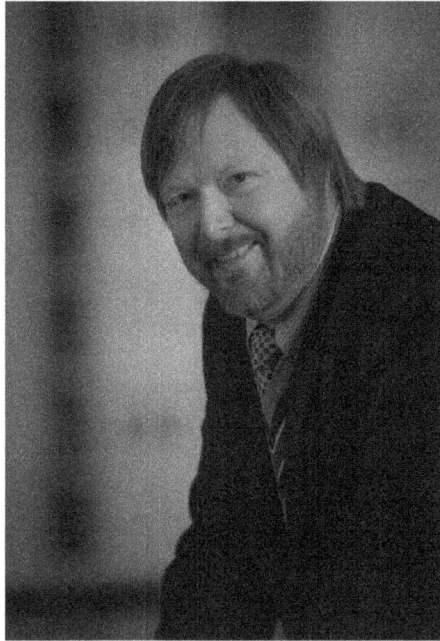

ABOUT THE AUTHOR

Dr. David A. Bishop is a technologist, systems/solutions architect, consultant, researcher, entrepreneur, and instructor with over 25 years of experience in telecommunications, transportation, airline, government, and utility industries. David holds a Bachelor of Computer Engineering degree from the Georgia Institute of Technology, an MBA with a concentration in IT management, and a Doctorate in Business Administration from Georgia State University. He is an inventor of five U.S. patents.

Dr. Bishop is the creator of agile vortex theory, which is the subject of his forthcoming book, *"Metagility: Managing Agile Development for Competitive Advantage"* and a regular contributor to engineering and management publications worldwide. He is a member and committee chair for the International Electrotechnical Commission based in Geneva, Switzerland, a member of the ACM, and a Senior Member of the **IEEE**.